HEALTHY FOR LIFE

Sex
AND
RELATIONSHIPS

Anna Claybourne

W
FRANKLIN WATTS
LONDON • SYDNEY

Franklin Watts
First published in Great Britain in 2016 by The Watts Publishing Group

Credits
Series editors: Sarah Peutrill and Sarah Ridley
Series designer and illustrator: Dan Bramall
Cover designers: Peter Scoulding and Cathryn Gilbert

ISBN 978 1 4451 4981 3
Printed in China

MIX
Paper from
responsible sources
FSC® C104740

**The publisher does not condone
or promote sexual relationships
between under-age individuals.**

Franklin Watts
An imprint of
Hachette Children's Group
Part of The Watts Publishing Group
Carmelite House
50 Victoria Embankment
London EC4Y 0DZ

An Hachette UK Company
www.hachette.co.uk

www.franklinwatts.co.uk

CONTENTS

Sex and relationships

When you're a child, you shouldn't have to think about sex and relationships. They are 'grown up' things that are only for adults.

But as you grow up, they can become very important. So, as you leave childhood and enter puberty, sex and relationships are a whole new area to learn about. This book is here to explain the basics – and give you the facts you need to know.

What is sex?

Sex is short for sexual intercourse, which is something that humans do in order to have babies, and for enjoyment.

To have sexual intercourse, people use their sex organs, which are found on the outside and the inside of their bodies. A man has a penis, and a woman has an opening between her legs called a vagina.

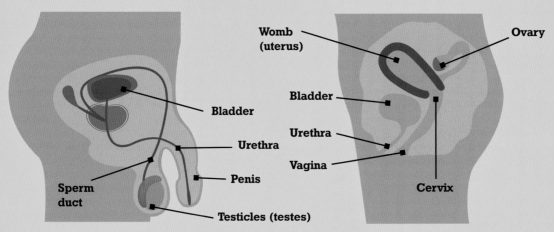

Male sex organs (side view)

- Bladder
- Urethra
- Penis
- Sperm duct
- Testicles (testes)

Female sex organs (side view)

- Womb (uterus)
- Ovary
- Bladder
- Urethra
- Vagina
- Cervix

During sexual intercourse, a man's penis will get hard. It fits into the woman's vagina. After sex, if a male sperm cell meets a female egg cell they may combine and may grow into a baby.

Sex for fun

Although people make babies by having sex, that's not the reason that most people have sex most of the time. Sex feels good and is a way to be close to a person you love or fancy. In fact, it's normal and natural to want to have sex – and for sex to take place, so long as both people feel the same way.

Other types of sex

There are other kinds of sex too. Sometime sex just means touching the sex organs in different ways.

Two men can have sex with each other.

So can two women.

Relationships

In this book, a relationship means love or involvement between people who are attracted to each other.

A relationship can be a long-term commitment between two people, like a marriage...

... or it can be something more casual, that only lasts a short time.

It can involve sex...

... or just kissing, hugging or being together.

Make it happy

As you grow up, it's important to learn how to handle relationships and sex in a healthy way, so you can:

- Stay physically healthy
- Say NO to being treated badly
- Make sex and relationships a happy, positive part of your life – if you want them.

Remember, it's also fine not to have sex or relationships if you don't want to, or if you don't feel ready.

Puberty and sex organs

From around the age of nine or ten, children's bodies go through a series of changes as they turn into adults. These changes are known as puberty.

During puberty, girls' and boys' bodies, including their sex organs or genitals, change on the outside, and on the inside. They do this so that when you are an adult, you will be able to have sex and have babies, if you want to. The changes are different in boys and girls.

Girls

Changes happen to the outside and the inside of a girl's body during puberty.

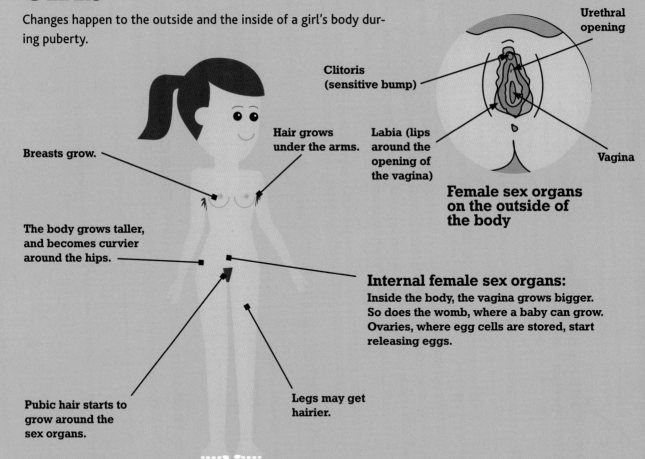

Breasts grow.

Hair grows under the arms.

The body grows taller, and becomes curvier around the hips.

Pubic hair starts to grow around the sex organs.

Legs may get hairier.

Clitoris (sensitive bump)

Labia (lips around the opening of the vagina)

Urethral opening

Vagina

Female sex organs on the outside of the body

Internal female sex organs:
Inside the body, the vagina grows bigger. So does the womb, where a baby can grow. Ovaries, where egg cells are stored, start releasing eggs.

Periods

Aound the age of 10 to 13, girls start having periods. Roughly each month, an ovary releases an egg and the womb builds up a thick lining of blood. This is where the egg could start to grow into a baby if the girl became pregnant. If that doesn't happen, the blood flows out of the vagina – and that's what we call a period.

Boys

Puberty brings changes to a boy's body on the outside and on the inside.

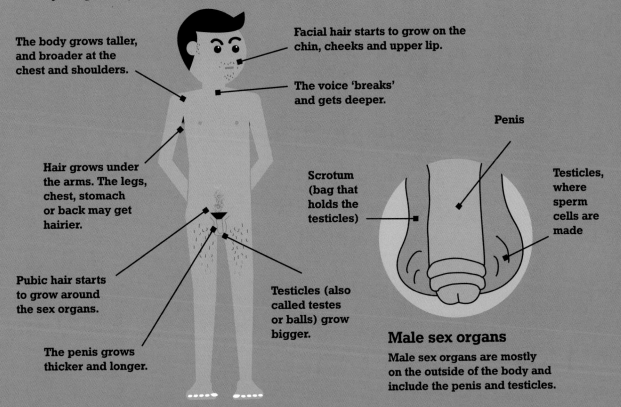

The body grows taller, and broader at the chest and shoulders.

Facial hair starts to grow on the chin, cheeks and upper lip.

The voice 'breaks' and gets deeper.

Hair grows under the arms. The legs, chest, stomach or back may get hairier.

Pubic hair starts to grow around the sex organs.

The penis grows thicker and longer.

Testicles (also called testes or balls) grow bigger.

Penis

Scrotum (bag that holds the testicles)

Testicles, where sperm cells are made

Male sex organs

Male sex organs are mostly on the outside of the body and include the penis and testicles.

Sexual feelings

As the sex organs change and grow, they can start to feel different and do some unfamiliar things. You can feel 'turned on' – an excited, tingly feeling in the sex organs. This can happen when you fancy someone or see or think about something sexual. Boys find their penis can get hard, or 'erect'.

Sometimes people experience an intense sexual feeling called orgasm, or 'coming'. When a boy has an orgasm, liquid called semen comes out of the penis. This is called ejaculating. It sometimes happens when a boy is asleep – this is called a 'wet dream'.

People may touch their own sex organs because it feels nice or causes an orgasm. This is called masturbation.

Sex organs and privacy

Sexual feelings, orgasms and masturbation are normal and natural. They are not wrong or bad for you. However, sex organs and sexual behaviour are private. Sex should only happen in private, between adults who agree to it.

Pregnancy

Pregnancy is the time when a woman has a baby growing inside her womb. Ideally, you will not have to deal with pregnancy until you choose to become a parent. To make sure that is the case, you need to know how it works!

How pregnancy happens

If a girl or woman has started her periods, she can get pregnant. For a pregnancy to start, a male sperm cell must join with a female egg cell, which can then start to grow inside the womb.

During sexual intercourse, semen from the penis enters the vagina. It is full of sperm that swim up through the womb and towards the ovaries. If an egg cell is present, the strongest sperm may fertilise the egg and it will embed itself in the lining of the womb.

A woman or girl is most likely to become pregnant during the days midway between one period and the next. However, it is not easy to know when this fertile time occurs. This means it is possible for someone to become pregnant during what she thought was a 'safe' time.

Womb (uterus)
Sperm
Egg
Ovary
Ovary
Sperm
Fallopian tube
Vagina

Preventing pregnancy

People often want to have sex and avoid pregnancy. To prevent it, they use contraception. There are several types of contraception. Although no contraceptive gives 100 per cent protection against pregnancy, most give 98 or 99 per cent protection.

Condom

This fits over the penis and catches the semen.

Cap or diaphragm

This is placed inside the vagina before sex to stop sperm entering the womb.

Pill

The girl or woman takes a daily pill that prevents pregnancy.

Pregnancy myths

You may hear lots of myths about what can and can't make you pregnant. Here are the facts!

Pregnancy CAN happen when people:
- Have sex standing up
- Wash out the vagina or have a wee after sex
- Have sex during a menstrual period
- Pull out the penis before orgasm
- Have sex underwater or in the bath
- Have sex for the first time.

These things do NOT cause pregnancy:
- Oral sex (touching the genitals with the mouth)
- Swallowing semen
- Masturbation.

Stopping a pregnancy

In some countries, if a pregnancy has started, it can sometimes be stopped with an operation or medicine. This is called an abortion or termination. Sometimes, pregnancies end on their own and do not continue. This is called a miscarriage.

Doctors, sexual health clinics and pharmacies can give advice on what to use and how it works.

The emergency contraceptive pill, also called the morning-after pill

This is a pill that can be taken up to five days after sex to prevent a pregnancy.

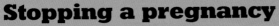

Coil

A device fitted inside the womb that prevents pregnancy.

Contraceptive injection, implant, patch or ring

These work like the pill but put the medicine into your body in other ways.

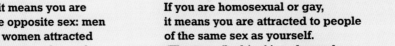

Sexuality and identity

Your sexuality means your sexual feelings and preferences. There are several types of sexuality.

Heterosexual or straight

If you are heterosexual, it means you are attracted to people of the opposite sex: men attracted to women, and women attracted to men. This is the most common form of sexuality.
In most surveys, over 80 per cent of people consider themselves straight.

Homosexual, gay, lesbian or queer

If you are homosexual or gay, it means you are attracted to people of the same sex as yourself. (The term 'lesbian' is only used for gay girls and women.)

Bisexual

Some people are bisexual, which means they are attracted to people of both sexes.

Asexual

If you are asexual it means you do not feel attracted to others in a sexual way – although you might still want a close, caring relationship.

Changing feelings

Sexuality can be 'fluid', or changeable. Some people's sexuality changes through their life. Others experiment with different things, especially when they are young, before deciding on their sexuality.

If you don't feel that you fit into any particular category, that's OK too.

Homophobia

Homophobia is the fear and hatred of homosexuality. It can lead to gay people being persecuted and attacked. Some traditional and religious views see homosexuality as abnormal or wrong. Gay sex used to be illegal in many parts of the world. In some countries, it still is – meaning that gay people can be charged with a crime and imprisoned.

Over time, this is changing. More and more people understand that different sexualities are normal, and they are now much more accepted in most places.

However, homophobic bullying does still happen. If you are attacked because of your sexuality, it's important to report it – and to remember that it is not your fault.

Coming out

Telling people, such as your family, friends or workmates, about your sexuality is known as 'coming out'. Some people are sure from an early age that they are gay, lesbian or transgender, while others might not come to that realisation until they are much older. It's your decision who you come out to, and when you decide to tell people.

I'd guessed.

That's a bit of a shock.

That's OK.

Transsexuality

Some people feel strongly that they were born in the wrong body. For example, if you were born in a female body but feel that you are a boy, or the other way around, you are transsexual or transgender.

It's possible to have a series of operations and hormone treatments to change your physical sex. This is called gender reassignment or a sex change. It is a very big step to take, so it's very important to be sure it's what you want. Transsexual or transgender people often change their name and spend some time living and dressing as the sex they feel they are, before making physical changes.

There are also some people who feel that they don't belong to either gender, male or female.

Crushes and dating

As you go through puberty, you may start to have feelings of love or attraction for other people. At some point, you might want to start having boyfriends or girlfriends.

A crush on you!

A 'crush' is a strong feeling of liking, fancying or loving someone. You might find yourself wanting to see them – or thinking about them – all the time. Younger children can have crushes, but during puberty they can really take over!

You can get crushes on all kinds of people...
... a friend,
... a classmate,
... a pop star or celebrity – or even a teacher!

Crushes can sometimes feel overwhelming. Daydreaming about your crush can be a major distraction.

If you do actually see the person, you can get embarrassed or tongue-tied.

Hi!

Oh... hey.

If the crush is on a teacher or other adult, or a celebrity, it can be upsetting, because you cannot have a relationship with them.

Starting relationships

On the plus side, if your crush is on a friend or a classmate, they might like you too!
During the teenage years, some people have their first boyfriends or girlfriends.
But what does that mean, exactly? It can mean a wide range of things.

At first, relationships are often just like close friendships.
You might hold hands and hang out together.

Kissing, 'snogging' or 'making out' is a way to be close to
your boyfriend or girlfriend. Sometimes people kiss with
their mouths open and touch their tongues together.

Touching each other's sex organs (petting) or actually
having sex are not an essential part of a relationship.
There are laws about how old you have to be before it is
OK to have sex (see page 18).

It's up to you!

Some of these things might sound scary and not something you want to do. That is fine.

Remember...

You do not have to do anything you don't want to do.

If the person you are with wants to do something and you don't, you can say no.
You can also end a relationship with a boyfriend or girlfriend whenever you
feel like it (for more on this, see page 16).

It's also fine and
normal to not have a
girlfriend or boyfriend
at all if you don't want
to, even if other friends
are in relationships.

Healthy relationships

Relationships are about being close to another person, loving them and caring about them, being kind to them, and having fun together.

What is a good, healthy relationship like?

Take a look at these features of a happy relationship to give you an idea.

Equal

Both the partners are equal, and just as important as each other. They take turns at things and share things fairly.

Respectful

Each person cares about the other person and their feelings. They try not to be rude, hurtful or critical.

Now tell me about your day.

Kind

The partners look after each other when they are sad, hurt or unwell. They do kind things for each other.

Free

Each person is free to live their own life, see their own friends and follow their own interests. If one person wants to leave or end the relationship, they can.

Have fun with your friends.

I'll see you at the weekend.

Falling out

In a relationship, it's normal to disagree sometimes, and even have arguments.

In a good relationship, though, people try to handle this in a reasonable way.

They try to:
Be honest about how they feel
Listen to what the other person has to say
Agree on solutions to problems together.

Take your time

During your teenage years, it's normal to have several different relationships. You do not have to settle down with your first boyfriend or girlfriend forever! Many people do not settle down with one other person until they are 25, 30 or even older.

If two people have been together for a long time, and are sure their relationship is permanent, they may want to start living together, or get married. Many people spend their lives as a couple. But again, there is no rush. And if you say yes to a commitment like this, you are always free to change your mind.

Having babies

In a long-term relationship, people may want to have children. Many people prefer to wait to have a baby until they are in a happy, stable relationship, so that they can share the cost, childcare and responsibility.

Although girls can get pregnant as soon they start having periods, it is also better for their bodies if they do not start having babies until they are older – from the age of about 18.

Relationship problems

Relationships are meant to be happy, friendly and loving – but that isn't always what happens. Sometimes, people behave badly in relationships, or they can go wrong in other ways.

When you're in a relationship, watch out for problems like these. They are signs that it's an unhealthy relationship that will not make you happy.

Jealousy

Not letting the other person talk to, or even look at, other boys or girls.

I don't like you looking at anyone else!

Controlling behaviour

Trying to control what the other person does.

I don't like you going to parties without me.

Emotional abuse or bullying

Putting the other person down, criticising them, saying mean and hurtful things, shouting, sulking or starting arguments on purpose.

You're stupid and ugly! I'm going to tell people you're boring.

Unfaithfulness

Kissing or having sex with someone else. (In most relationships, people agree to only have a relationship with each other.)

Inequality or sexism

Expecting the other person to do all the work, or behave a certain way just because they are male or female.

She always expects me to pay, even though neither of us has much money.

Violence

Any kind of violence (such as hitting, kicking, pushing or pinching), or threatening violence, is not OK.

No thanks!

You are free to end a relationship that isn't making you happy. You don't need to think of a reason to end it. Saying, "I don't want to be in this relationship," is enough.

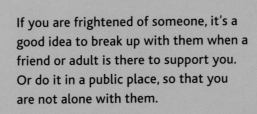

It's just me. I really need to talk to you about Rob and me. I'm not happy...

If you want to break up with someone and they try to make it difficult for you, or threaten you, you don't have to give in. You can talk to an adult you trust, and ask for help.

If you are frightened of someone, it's a good idea to break up with them when a friend or adult is there to support you. Or do it in a public place, so that you are not alone with them.

Getting dumped

Even happy relationships can come to an end, especially when you're young. If you love someone and they break up with you, accepting that the relationship is over can be really hard. These ideas might help.

Look after yourself and try to eat and sleep well.

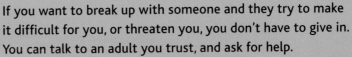

Talk to someone about your feelings – a friend, parent or relative you trust.

Spend time doing fun things with friends, and enjoying sports, hobbies or days out.

It might not feel like it at first, but you will get over it.

Healthy sex

As you grow up, it's normal to wonder when you should have sex for the first time, and what sex is really like (or should be like!).

The age of consent

Firstly, you should know the age of consent where you live. Most countries have laws about how old you must be before you can legally have sex – usually somewhere around 16.

The laws may be different for heterosexual sex and homosexual or gay sex.

When you're ready

You should only have sex if both people want it. You should feel relaxed and happy about it, and not pressured into it. It's best to talk about it first so that you both know how the other person feels. And don't forget to talk about contraception (see pages 8–9).

We've talked about sex and I'm ready.

Me too.

Giving your consent

'Consent' means agreement. Another person should only have sex with you if you consent, or agree. Once you have consented, though, that still doesn't mean you have to go through with it.

• You can change your mind at any time.

• Even if you are having sex, you can still say no and ask the other person to stop.

What is it like?

So, once you're sure you want to, and it's not illegal – how does sex actually work?

People usually kiss, hug and touch each other before sex. This is called foreplay. It helps people to get turned on – more interested in sex. For a boy or man, the penis gets erect and ready for sex. For a girl or a woman, the vagina relaxes and becomes wetter, making sex easier to do.

Especially at first, it helps to be slow and careful. No one should be rough or get hurt.

During sexual intercourse between a man and a woman (or a boy and a girl), the boy or man pushes or 'thrusts' his penis into the girl's or woman's vagina. This should feel nice for both people, and shouldn't hurt. Sex usually ends when one or both people have had an orgasm – although this doesn't always happen.

Safe sex

Sexual intercourse can spread diseases, known as sexually transmitted diseases or sexually transmitted infections (STDs or STIs). These include AIDS, chlamydia, herpes, gonorrhoea, syphilis, and crabs or pubic lice.

To avoid STDs and STIs, it's best to always use a condom, as well as any other contraception you may be using (see pages 8–9). Condoms fit over the penis, so they prevent sperm from entering the girl's or woman's body, and also help to stop germs spreading from one person to the other.

Putting on a condom

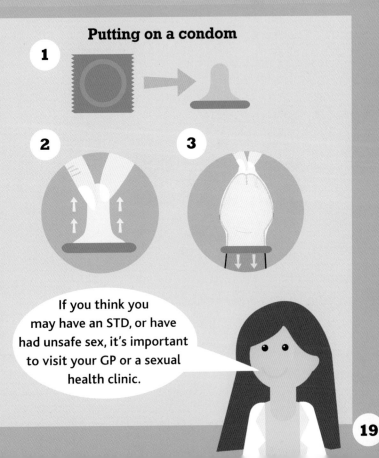

1

2

3

If you think you may have an STD, or have had unsafe sex, it's important to visit your GP or a sexual health clinic.

Under pressure

People can sometimes feel that they should have sex when they don't really want to, because of pressure put on them by others.

Pressure from your partner

If you're in a relationship with someone, they should care about your feelings, and not pressure you to have sex. But it can happen. Your partner might say something like:

> You would if you really loved me.

> I'll break up with you if you don't.

> If you won't, I'll tell people you're frigid.*

> My friends will laugh at me if I'm a virgin.**

* Frigid is a hurtful word that means cold, or not interested in sex.

** And a virgin is someone who has never had sex.

But you don't have to have sex just because someone else is putting pressure on you to do so. If they don't care about how you feel, and what you want, you don't need to be with them at all. So what can you say? It's fine to say something like:

> OK, maybe I don't love you that much then.

> OK. I would rather break up than have sex when I'm not ready.

> What your friends think of me is not my problem.

> If you're happy to spread gossip about me, I don't think you love me any more.

> Remember, there are plenty of people out there to go out with. You don't need to stay with someone who puts pressure on you.

Peer pressure

Your peers are people a similar age to you, such as friends and schoolmates.
In schools, there's often a lot of gossip about sex, and who might or might not have had it. It might surprise you to learn that a lot of people lie about having had sex. People sometimes feel they should have sex so that others will admire them or look up to them.

If you don't want to have sex, you can get called:

frigid *prudish* uptight

On the other hand, if people think you are having sex, you can get called:

easy loose *a slut* a slag

Either way, these insults are not fair! You get to decide what happens to your body, and what other people think does not need to affect that.

Rape, assault and abuse

People sometimes try to make someone have sex with them by simply going ahead and trying to force them into it. Or they may do sexual things with someone they have power over, such as a child. These things are serious crimes.

Is it rape?

Rape means making someone have sex without their consent. So what counts as rape?

It is also rape if a penis or other object is put into the bottom (anus), rather than the vagina, without consent.

The victim does not actually have to say 'no'. It's common for them to freeze in fear and not say anything. But if they have not clearly consented, it is still rape.

It is possible for men and boys to be raped, as well as girls and women.

Sexual assault and harassment

There are also other types of illegal sexual behaviour. They may be classed as sexual assault, indecent assault or sexual harassment. They include:

• Touching someone's sex organs without their consent

• Grabbing, groping, kissing or touching someone in a sexual way without their consent

• Making obscene or sexual remarks to someone that upset them.

I know you want sex.

Help!
I didn't know he felt like this.

After an attack

If someone has been raped or sexually assaulted, they can feel very, very upset, depressed, or even ashamed (even though they have not done anything wrong). It's important to tell someone and get medical help and support as soon as possible, and to report the attack to the police, even though this may be frightening.

Hello? I'd like to report a rape.

Rape and sexual assault can cause injuries, emotional problems and STDs or STIs. A doctor can help.

Sexual abuse

Forcing sexual activity on someone is often called sexual abuse, especially if the victim is under the age of consent (usually the age of 16). Unfortunately, this does happen. Children and young people are sometimes sexually abused by a family friend or relative, a teacher, religious leader or club leader, a sibling, or even a parent or grandparent.

The abuser may act in one or more of these ways.

• Tell the victim that the abuse is a secret.
• Try to make the victim feel special and loved, or that they are their 'boyfriend' or 'girlfriend'.
• Threaten the victim that if they tell, they will hurt them or their family.
• Tell the victim that it's their fault and people will blame them.

However, if you or someone you know is experiencing sexual abuse, it's not the victim's fault and you can report it. If you can tell a kind, trustworthy teacher, family member, friend or doctor, they will be able to help.

Sex and technology

Young people growing up today have to deal with things that their parents had never heard of when they were teenagers! The Internet, smartphones and texting can all make sex and relationships even more complicated.

Sex texts and photos

Long ago, people in a relationship could only chat in person, on the phone or in a letter. Today, we use emails, texts and social media, and we can send photos instantly or chat via webcam. So some people use this technology to send things like texts about their sex life or relationship, or naked or 'nudie' photos or videos of themselves or their sex organs.

The problem is – it can be hard to keep these things private!
- It's easy to copy a text, photo or video and send it to other people.
- It can be posted on the Internet for the whole world to see.
- Once something's appeared on a social networking site, it can be very hard to delete.

What can you do?

Young people often feel under pressure to share things like sexual photos, videos and texts. And you may want to do these things. Before you do, though, remember that anything you send could one day be shared with the whole school – or the whole world – for years into the future. Once it is out there, you have no control over your material.

Ask yourself whether you would want these people to see what you've sent:

Your parents or grandparents

Your favourite teacher

A future employer

The children you might have one day

If the answer is NO, think twice. Remember you don't HAVE to do anything, online or in real life, that you don't want to.

Safety online

Internet chat rooms and social media mean you can talk to anyone online. Some people use this to try to make friends with young people in order to sexually abuse them.

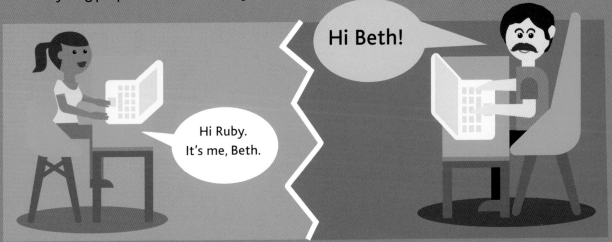

For this reason, it's best to:

Keep parents informed about who you are chatting to.
Never share photos, personal information, your address or other identifying details online, unless you can control your privacy settings so that only friends you've met see them.
On public sites, always use a made-up nickname or username, not your real name.
Avoid meeting up in real life with anyone you have met online.
If anyone online behaves oddly, puts pressure on you, or asks for photos, tell an adult.

Online porn

Porn (short for pornography) means pictures or films of people doing sexual things.
People often watch it in order to get turned on before masturbating or having sex.
There is lots of porn on the Internet.

Porn can give people a distorted idea of what sex and other people's bodies should be like.
It can show people being treated badly during sex too. This can lead to some people
expecting sex in real life to resemble the porn they have seen.

Remember...

Your body does NOT have to look like people in porn films.
You do NOT have to do anything just because it happens in porn.
You do not EVER have to watch porn yourself if you don't want to.

Healthy for life

Sex and relationships are an important part of most people's lives. Make them respectful, loving and safe, and you'll help to make them a healthy, happy part of your life too.

It's your choice

Your body is yours, and you are the boss of what happens to it. It's your life and your future, and you get to decide what you want to do.

You have the right to make your own decisions when it comes to sex and relationships, about what to do, and who to do it with.

Having a boyfriend or girlfriend

Having sexual intercourse or choosing not to

Other sexual activities

Coming out

Getting married

Having children

You have a right not to be sexually harassed, abused, assaulted or intimidated, or treated badly in relationships.

You have a right to privacy regarding your body, sex life and relationships.

Safe and healthy

Whatever your sexuality, safe sex will help to make sure you stay healthy. Unless you are trying to have a baby with someone you trust and know well, the best way to keep sex safe, and avoid catching a sexually transmitted disease, is to use a condom every time.

Remember – to have sex, you need consent

Sex cannot be happy and healthy if one of the people involved did not agree to it. If you want sex and you are not sure if the other person consents, ask them! It's not enough to just assume someone else will be OK with it.

- Have they said yes?
- Are they happy and enthusiastic about having sex?
- Did they agree without any pressure being put on them?
- Are they asleep, unconscious or affected by alcohol or drugs?
- If they are, they cannot give consent properly, so you cannot have sex with them.

More questions?

A short book like this can't include everything you might want to know about sex and relationships as you grow up. It's an introduction to give you the basic facts, but you may have more questions. There are other books, websites and resources that can help too. You can find some of these listed on page 31. You can also ask your doctor or a trusted parent or family member about things you want to know.

After all, the more you know and understand about sex and relationships, the better! Knowing what they should be like means you'll know if something is wrong. Learning all about contraception, safe sex and respectful relationships is the best way to make sex and relationships as good as they can be for you – for the rest of your life.

Have a happy, healthy future!

Contraception	How it works	Effectiveness*
Condom	A thin cover that fits over the man's penis to stop sperm escaping.	98 per cent effective
Pill	A daily pill taken by the woman, containing a drug that prevents pregnancy.	99 per cent effective
Cap or diaphragm	A rubber dome that fits over the woman's cervix (the entrance to the womb) to stop sperm getting in.	92-96 per cent effective
Female condom	A thin cover that fits inside the woman's vagina to stop sperm reaching the womb.	95 per cent effective
Coil or IUD (intrauterine device)	A device that is kept inside the woman's womb on a long-term basis to prevent a pregnancy starting.	Over 99 per cent effective
Contraceptive injection, implant, patch or ring	Drugs that prevent a woman getting pregnant, introduced into the woman's body using an injection, an implant under the skin, a skin patch, or a ring inserted into the vagina.	Over 99 per cent effective
Emergency contraceptive pill or MAP (morning-after pill)	A pill containing a drug that prevents a pregnancy, taken by the woman up to five days after unprotected sex has taken place.	Variable, according to when it is taken
Rhythm method or natural family planning	This means only having sex at certain times of the woman's menstrual cycle (cycle of periods), when she is least likely to get pregnant.	Around 75 per cent effective
Withdrawal	This means starting to have sex, but stopping before the man comes or ejaculates. It is not very effective as sperm can escape before ejaculation.	Around 70 per cent effective
Sterilisation	Either the man or the woman, or both, can have permanent operations that prevent sperm or eggs from being released, so they cannot meet up.	Over 99 per cent effective
No method	If a couple don't use any type of contraception at all, there's around an 85 per cent chance of pregnancy within a year.	

*The effectiveness rating shows how many couples will avoid a pregnancy in a year of using the method. For example, condoms are about 98 per cent effective. This means that if 100 couples use condoms for a year, about 98 of them will not get pregnant, but two couples probably will.

Always use a condom

The chart opposite shows the effectiveness of contraception methods at preventing a pregnancy. However, it's very important to always use a condom when having sex, including gay sex, to prevent the spread of germs that can cause sexually transmitted diseases or infections (STDs/STIs). Even if you are also using another method of contraception, you should use a condom.

Sexual health clinics and GPs can give advice on what types of contraception might be best for you, and how to use them.

Sex and pregnancy myths

You might hear people saying all kinds of things about what can and can't cause pregnancy. Many of them are myths. Check them out here to see what the real truth is.

"You can't get pregnant the first time you have sex."
MYTH. Any sexual intercourse can lead to pregnancy.

"You can't get pregnant if you only have sex once."
MYTH. Any sexual intercourse can lead to pregnancy.

"You can't get pregnant if the man pulls out before he comes."
MYTH. Sperm can leak out and cause pregnancy, even before the man comes.

"You can't get pregnant if you have sex during your period."
MYTH. Women have become pregnant this way.

"You can't get pregnant if you have sex standing up."
MYTH. You can get pregnant whatever position you use for sexual intercourse.

"You can't get pregnant if you have sex in the bath, or wash your vagina out afterwards."
MYTH. Neither of these things will stop sperm being able to enter the womb.

"You can make a condom from cling film or a plastic bag."
MYTH. This won't work as these things are not designed for sex, and will leak or break (as well as being very uncomfortable).

"You can wash a condom out and re-use it."
MYTH. This isn't a good idea as re-using a condom makes it more likely to break, and you might not get rid of all the sperm. You need a new condom each time you have sex.

"A boy's balls will explode/be damaged if he doesn't have sex."
MYTH. If sperm is not used, the boy's or man's body absorbs it and gets rid of it. The balls (testicles) cannot 'over-fill' with sperm. Boys and men can also masturbate if they want to – they do not need to have sex.

On the other hand...

"You can't get pregnant from oral sex."
TRUE. Oral sex (touching the sex organs with the mouth or tongue) cannot, on its own, lead to pregnancy – even if the woman swallows some sperm.

"You can't get pregnant from masturbation."
TRUE. Masturbation cannot lead to pregnancy, as long as your hands are clean and have not been touching sperm.

Glossary

abortion Ending a pregnancy deliberately by medical treatment.

abuse Cruel, violent or hurtful treatment.

asexual Not feeling any sexual feelings or attraction.

bisexual Sexually attracted to both your own and the opposite sex.

coming Another word for having an orgasm.

coming out Telling people that you are gay or transgender.

consent Agreement or permission.

contraception Methods of preventing pregnancy.

egg (cell) A cell released from a woman's ovaries, which can grow into a baby if it combines with a sperm cell.

ejaculation This happens when semen comes out of the penis, usually during orgasm.

erection This happens when a boy or man feels turned on and his penis becomes stiff.

fertilisation A sperm cell combining with an egg cell so that it can grow into a baby.

foreplay Kissing and touching before having sex.

gay Another word for homosexual.

genitals Sex organs that can be seen on the outside of the body.

heterosexual Being sexually attracted to the opposite sex from yourself.

homophobia Hatred or fear of homosexual people, sometimes involving abusive behaviour.

homosexual Being sexually attracted to the same sex as yourself.

lesbian A name for a female homosexual.

making out Another name for kissing.

masturbation Touching or rubbing your own genitals because it feels good.

menstrual cycle The repeated sequence of a woman's body releasing eggs and having periods.

orgasm An intense sexual feeling in the genitals.

ovaries Two organs inside a woman's body that release egg cells.

peer pressure Pressure from your peers (friends, schoolmates or people a similar age to you) to behave in particular ways.

period A flow of blood and womb lining from the vagina, roughly once a month.

porn Images or films of sex organs or sexual activity, designed to act as a turn-on.

pregnant Having a baby growing inside the womb.

puberty Series of physical changes that make a child become an adult.

pubic hair Hair that grows around the genitals from puberty onwards.

queer Another word for homosexual or bisexual.

rape Forcing another person to have sex, which is a serious crime.

safe sex Having sex in a way that prevents germs being passed on, such as using a condom.

semen The liquid that surrounds sperm cells as they leave the penis.

sexual abuse Making someone take part in sexual activity, especially someone younger or less powerful.

sexual assault An incident of sexual

behaviour or touching forced on another person against their will.

sexual harassment Making unwanted sexual comments or advances.

sexual intercourse Having sex in which the man's penis enters the woman's vagina.

sexuality A person's sexual preferences, or the things that turn them on.

snogging Another name for kissing.

sperm (cell) A cell released from a man's testes, which can grow into a baby if it combines with an egg cell.

STD/STI (short for sexually transmitted disease or infection) Disease or infection spread by sexual contact.

straight Another word for heterosexual.

termination Another name for an abortion.

testes/testicles Two male organs below the penis that produce sperm; also called balls.

transgender Feeling that you are a different gender or sex than the body you were born into.

transsexual A word sometimes used in the same way as transgender.

unprotected sex Having sex without using contraception to prevent pregnancy, or a condom to prevent STDs/STIs.

unsafe sex Another name for unprotected sex.

vagina The tube in a woman's or girl's body leading to the womb.

wet dream This happens when a boy or man has an orgasm and ejaculates while asleep.

womb The organ inside a woman's body where a baby can live and grow before birth.

 # Further information

Books and websites

Asking About Sex & Growing Up
by Joanna Cole, HarperCollins, 2009

Sex, Snogs, Dates and Mates
by Anita Naik, Wayland, 2013

Usborne Growing Up for Boys
by Alex Frith, Usborne Publishing, 2013

Usborne Growing Up for Girls
by Felicity Brooks, Usborne Publishing, 2013

Teenshealth: Love and Romance
http://kidshealth.org/en/teens/love.html

Planned Parenthood: Info for Teens
https://www.plannedparenthood.org/teens

Brook (advice on sexual health, relationships and wellbeing)
https://www.brook.org.uk/your-life

Rape Crisis (support for victims of rape, sexual abuse or sexual assault)
http://rapecrisis.org.uk/

NOTE TO PARENTS AND TEACHERS:
Every effort has been made by the Publishers to ensure that these websites are suitable for children, that they are of the highest educational value, and that they contain no inappropriate or offensive material. However, because of the nature of the Internet, it is impossible to guarantee that the contents of these sites will not be altered. We strongly advise that Internet access is supervised by a responsible adult.

Index